BILLACK'S
BONES

JOANNA GUTHRIE

BILLACK'S BONES

To Natalie

Hope you enjoy!

Best wishes

Jo G.

A *The Rialto*
First Edition

June 2015

ACKNOWLEDGEMENTS

Several of these poems have appeared in recent issues of The Rialto. *'Oilskins'* and *'Afternoon, Carn Brea'* first appeared in Exeter Flying Post in 2006.

The author is directly indebted to Alice Oswald for two poems in this collection. The long-titled *'Stork Hill, Little Tor Orchard, Duck Egg Field, Coffins Meadow, Cross Foot and Great Well Down,'* and *'Ten Commandments For The Rain'* were both generated in a workshop she ran in Ivybridge, Devon, in 2005.

The author would like to give particular thanks to Rose and to Rachel for their support and encouragement over the years.

First Published in 2007

The Rialto, PO Box 309, Aylsham, Norwich, England NR11 6LN

© Joanna Guthrie

ISBN 978-0-9551273-0-4

The publisher acknowledges financial assistance from the Arts Council of England, East.

The Rialto is a Registered Charity No. 297553

Typeset in Berling Roman 10pt on 13pt leading

Design and artwork by Starfish, Norwich.

Cover image by the Author

Printed by Micropress Limited, Halesworth, Suffolk.

To my family, to Andy, and to W.B.

CONTENTS

London Dream   8
Billack Writes His Memoirs   9
The Moon   11
From a Marble   12
Greener II   13
Ten Commandments for the Rain   14
May 5   15
Bluebag   16
Titanic 1999   17
Summer Solstice, Fifth Year of the Current Intifada   18
Like Scraps of Cloth Cheeps Blink   19
The Pitchfork   20
Hot Air Balloon   21
Afternoon, Carn Brea   23
Telegraph Poles   24
June   25
The Weather   26
Stork Hill, Little Tor Orchard, Duck Egg Field, Coffins   27
Meadow, Cross Foot and Great Well Down
The Child's Shoe Up The Chimney   28
Nine Maidens   29
Singing Bowl   30
The Journey of Milk   32
City   33

Oilskins   34
The Polystyrene Theme Park   36
Tea Strainer   37
The Mirror in the Palace in Bhuj   38
Clouds   39
Days In   40
CCTV   41
Paul   42
BS 3   43
Kathmandu   44
Samhain   45
New Year's Day Balloons   47
In Their Garden, After The Osteopath   48
Your Science   49
Cigarette Farmyard, 1 a.m.   50
At Blakeney Point   51
What Happened In Little Tor Orchard   52
The Fisherwoman In The Painting   53
Eden   54
Headfirst   55
Thing   56
For My Sister's Eighteenth Birthday   57
Billack's Bones   58
Coda   63

LONDON DREAM

We rowed through star porridge.
How was it?
As you'd expect:
sweet to the touch
speckled, stirred with light
smooth and bottomless.
You dived for a shell,
blue-lidded. Surfaced with it,
your head webbed with silver spawn.
The blue shell held
my explanations, you said ,
but I woke, then -
to a prehistoric cave,
lying under red sheepskin.
Woke again -
staring in to a goat's yellow scored eyes.
And woke again -
here, with the traffic
and the pink sky.

BILLACK WRITES HIS MEMOIRS

'I lay', wrote Billack, 'perhaps years to write this.'
Settled down by the powdery tree,
spreading, and pulled from his pocket
a watch
which told him the time
was to begin.
Mouthing the words, he wrote. Time settled.

A howl crept up to look.
The stars picked him out,
mountain rivulets bowing his head
as he pushed his pen.
Animals still around him,
silence while the world waited
his story. There were visions and noises

stored up in him - every hole in his head
had sucked them in, or in they'd drifted
to his speckled sieve
of blindness and sight.
There were lilies at night,
some place – he'd stood
and stared: they'd peeked

above him in star shape,
taut white triangles
that perfumed the dark.

Another day, he'd seen bees like kittens,
so fur-heavy and fat: filling the yard
with their buzzing.
And kittens like women,
demanding and delicate.
They had astonished him
with sharp-chinned beauty.
Something else Billack remembered:
a bird and a drum.
In a valley once, their voices -
the rhythms built and matched
and hung together like layered lace.
He stopped here.

Had they heard each other?
Was it the truth
that a bird's flute
and a drum beat
could mesh so well that music climbed the sky?
His pen dropped like moss.
Billack saw all, knew nothing.

THE MOON

It looks like bone polished to silver, as usual.
It has a bouncing double through a trick of the glass
which hangs from its lap like an apron
and this pastel bluebell-blue encircling it.
Maybe a larger ring too, of red-purple, like old blackcurrant.
I am privileged to have it shining into my bedroom,
standing at the back of the scenery,
at the top of an invisible mountain, ready to come
rolling down, like a marble down a run,
and crack through the glass,
fluttering the curtains and landing on the bed,
about the size of a penny it would be.

FROM A MARBLE

For a minute, you are held
in the slippery belly of the earth
where there is a parting of rock -
it levers you down
to heal
without eyes open.

Combed green slime licks round your skin,
pressed from the frown of folded valley:
the near gripping stone, which is your seat
and ceiling,
walls and door.

For some seconds you are squeezed
into this air pocket of a wild-streaked marble.

These breathing rooms

exist for you
to cool, as you lie with stored strata,
pulling stewed air   from the pause in density.
Creases wink at you. In the compression, stretch -

outside you waits the universe,
the hole which holds our weight.

GREENER II

Ecstatic pupil, don't you see
the limbering up, the limbs, the tree?
Too flighty
in all green-garbed tone
it suffers and can't see
the bone.
The merriment
which brings the din
you sit within
is telling you
a prayer. It's only one small step
a skin
to push through
like a paper drum,
a fiddle's dragging hum
which arches your foot and cocks your head
to side – there: before you know it, you
up the tree, sitting
with bright eyes.
Your hair stands on end
and points to the sky, like each young branch.
The sound you hear is every bird
and insect
and scraping wing, making.
They would be silent if you were not here –
nowhere for
their spits to bounce. Too clear.
The web we weave holds us between
the earth and sky. Climb now, there are plenty of spaces.

TEN COMMANDMENTS FOR THE RAIN

Fall forgivingly.
Rinse us again and again.

Temper your moods,
gather purity from hidden pools,

never desert us.
Cool the cities, the smoking pans.

Give rise to grass richer than chocolate.
Let us near you.

Hide and replenish yourself at the mouth of the sky.
Laugh on us.

MAY 5

The turbine turns, its three limbs bowl
air over arm repeatedly,
and this air fills our day,
and poplar lines shine lime-ily

in a beaming green grid which stands like a room
of expectant party people
in their fresh fiesta best
who wait, with me not up for it, not dressed.

BLUEBAG

Paint me with a blue brush.
Let the bristles drip with that
indigo, bluebell blue, and please
soak it into my spine, softly,
stroke it in even lengths
over my body, very wet
and definite. The blue

will percolate through my skin,
my nails, my face, will wash
my blood a blue tide, my larynx
a cornflower, my heart a mill of sky,
your brush licking persistent
and dipping, dipping, into the sweet
deep bucket which carries the sea, the change.

TITANIC, 1999

We drown ourselves until sleep,
sleep and dream, to drown.
Kill with dreams of sleeping,
inject our dreams, which drown us.

We cry at a drowning of love,
we dream of a flood covering our heads.
Our thoughts pour up to a fiery sky.
We depress and shrug under.

Our ship's bigger than it ever was,
on a rolling hand of lights and time.
The next wave's coming, to push away our homes,
we think: our heads will be covered by nothing.

SUMMER SOLSTICE, FIFTH YEAR
OF THE CURRENT INTIFADA

All night I dreamed it was day, and light
all night; dreamt of it being and staying light.
My body kept track as the light shifted,
as grains of day poured in early to blot the night.

In these dreams, I walked and laughed
with you, my sister, past the City Hall. We talked
about how there were only two choices:
light or dark. How life was that simple.
This seemed hilarious to us.

The air stung a little, there on the City Hall steps.
It flicked me, as if to say: your kind,
you will decay, eventually, from all this exposure,
this dark to light and back again.
Like a train flashes through tunnels until it wears out,
a moth swings round a bulb shaving particles from itself,
a bat collects phosphorescent moss –
as you drink it in, it wears you thin.
But carry on.

All night I was filled
with these pale hallucinations.
My eyelids glowed like pearls.
When it was morning,
I poured milk into coffee. The windows
hung in an abundance of white.

LIKE SCRAPS OF CLOTH CHEEPS BLINK

As birds come whistling and flute and croon like
jazz, the caw of a voice cracks over the field.
It bounces across the ridges. Wind slides through:
a belly – gathers before and draws behind: a sweep.
Sweet, pineful breaths of living air
bare themselves and wait, into the season.

As birdsong stitches fat air like a blanket,
a bark break, and swallows whole itself, no more.
The sky spreads down, an open-mouthed heart,
to lead, and press its muscles on the leaves
which have such baby bones they do no bleeding.
And little legs and stalks walk round to feel it.

THE PITCHFORK

Then he enticed me into the fair –
and I said I would go on the parachutes
where we could drift diagonally like spores,
graze the ground with just a gentle mooning in the stomach,
but he told me to come with him on to the fastest
where it throws and hurtles
and circles at angles: I could trust him,
he said, it would be fine,
definitely – and we were locked in
and when it grew fast, he said, it will get faster

and the world pulsed past in uneven rushes,
the music trailing behind, my head
knocking on its stalk, I clenched
against the air, smelling red metal
and he said, let go –

HOT AIR BALLOON

Under the night we lay, only nylon
but a skein of silk, your canvas swashed
about us, hung, like long green hair.

The tent was like a corn husk,
a rounded body dried empty by the sun,
guyed down where it mattered, to stop us

from floating absently away: unzipping
to find ourselves in Egypt.
There is a limit. 4 a.m.,

I sat and wriggled out to stand and stretch –
two heels on scuffed combed grass. Ash-silver garden
plating away. Only I and the house standing

at that hour. One sound: breeze pushing air.
By my knee, domed in by the bright green breast,
you slept. How useful, to be sheathed

from this by only this: to slip
out, in, uninvited – melt into
our night as our garden, into loud

flat curled fields, into meaty cliffs
and singing sea. I'd pierced in,
black thread through a needle, not even waking it

with a doorclick. Metallic grass glinted,
felt fur to my soles, and the volts
from the Earth knocked me over –

though I stood, a lone pole, then I knelt again,
unzipped back: a billowing skin snaked into
the room without day name, with you.

You were blond as dry sand, you sighed
when you touched me, palming gritty weight,
clutched me, in dumb regret at this cell

we'd cultivated quickly, in the green glob.
We surfaced less often: we were slipping –
on nylon floor, on shooting earth,

in tugging seaweed. It's wet in there
and there's no cure. In the morning
the house was back. I walked inside.

We went about forgetting. In daylight,
who knows what lurks and laughs
in sly eclipsing shafts

of high enchanting strength,
waiting only for some dark,
a roof, a name.

AFTERNOON, CARN BREA

They skid through the air of the village
while kids on bikes and men with sticks
slide down the lane in slow motion.
I see them dip to a tree,
in the field, back of our house.
They take it.. The rooks control the shade, the sun,
the space above our streets, which keeps
our heads pressed down.
Which makes us look up.
The grass glints hard – it glares
in stand-off with the sun, and now the rooks
make tracks: oiled wings slice deep
over my bright lawn, slick black against the green -
there are twenty,
they know I'm watching. They don't need to look.
I couldn't go near them, flying gang. They leave
suddenly: they'll be back when they like.

TELEGRAPH POLES

For birds, I thought, at four, at six, at nine,
when you sculpt your own sense
from what's around you
and don't think to ask but just continue

to watch and gaze, half-seeing them, at sea.
You can't crack codes, you do not try,
just follow your grown-up down the road
past men with beards who drink on the wall

into the meat shop, with its fat bright pinks
and froth of white frills on a slab
where an old woman gives you sugar fags.
Your grown-up speaks to her, you stand and stare,

then tag along below the even poles
which rise up bleached and stout
to the daylight.
Their scarred wood sprouts from pavement. Not quite tree,

it reaches up to a nest of knobs
and short iron branches, for birds to roost
or fly from. A crown of lines
stretches to sunset past the tower blocks,

the swollen shape of a big top's ceiling.
Brown birds are studded all the way across
to have a chat, or gaze, half-seeing us,
as their trapeze billows with dirty air

shoots over the chimneys,
scrapes the roof of the street.
They anchor it importantly, in rows,
and hide in darkness, I thought, for a snooze.

Those nights, I'd dream of a skinny ladder
that propped itself solid against a sky
which I would climb alone without stopping,
in thin brightness, extraordinary high.

JUNE

See how skilfully the hawk tilts, checks, tips,
to keep herself a still flat, bound
by air and over the
elderflowers catapulting dust,
the full-throated trees.

How she hangs, balancing.

I am down,
grinding through tarmac.
I practice with my hand
lifted to the window;
glide and tremble a thumb;
fill with the burn of muscle control.
It is steely discipline, to rise above.
It requires all my attention.

THE WEATHER

The birds congregate to speak about the weather.
They prong the ground and there is loose talk
caught by a wind that jingles the leaves
and shakes our bones, and they call and bounce,
they prong the ground, and there is loose talk.

My secrets whisper across the river
and shake my bones, they call and bounce.
My lips crowd the oak's familiar leather,
my secrets whisper across the bark
and all the trees say 'Shh, shh,' discreetly.

My lips crowd the oak's familiar leather
but the wood can take it.
The trees say 'Shh' insistently
and the birds call thoughts about the wind
but the woods can take it

and the park sleeps and I call for my love
and the birds call thoughts about the wind
and wind their bones across the ground
so the park sleeps and I call for my love
to hear me, and whisper my worries,

caught by a wind that jangles the leaves,
that files down my words to their stubby roots, and
the birds might meet to speak about the weather.

STORK HILL, LITTLE TOR ORCHARD, DUCK EGG FIELD, COFFINS MEADOW, CROSS FOOT AND GREAT WELL DOWN

In Coffins Meadow you lie and I wait for you
all night long with the weight of the load
pressing against my shoulders in ribbons
of knotted hot grievances ready to show.

In Little Tor Orchard we crushed the dock leaves
as I curled my feet to the peppery floor –
last year's black apples hiding around us
and a late wasp nosed close near my wrist.

Duck Egg Field was where you took me
to paddle the shadows of Stork Hill.
Your feet floated delicate in the wash of pooled gold,
gliding over the pebbles like a dream.

We walked Cross Foot in darkness
and squeezed into Coffins Meadow
beside your mother's house. Now you sleep
and won't believe you've dreamt, when daylight wakes you.

When daylight noses against your skin
like a wasp's movement brings cool air, you'll lift
your chin to shake clear of the purple
and you won't come with me to Great Well Down.

THE CHILD'S SHOE UP THE CHIMNEY

Beside the hearth, where the bricks spiral round themselves,
beside the hearth clogged with breakings of ash
and drifts of Christmas,
he squirrels his arm in, one evening,
to the cave, where the dark blinks
and four centuries sit, sealed in their silent temper.
He lets his fingers stretch
and touch a sense of something:
the edge of a footstep, caught full pelt.

He delivers it in a cold dribble of dust –
she lies puckered in his palm, a fledgling,
a sheath of parched kid, squirreled away
one evening when the space was fresh,
when the bricks lined up heavy on one another
ready to begin their melody;
to hold the dark off,
to let the fire wink,
while her shoe left a foothold for grace.

The raw bricks scraped a long stripe past his wrist –
the red of new leather, blood like a woman
can lend to a man
from the centre of things.
He kneels, and tells himself: don't get involved
in filing and tripping on ghosts.

NINE MAIDENS

Old stone, you smell of
pressed dust held fast and close and cold.
You smell of a spark: the trapped nerve
which divides you, quarters you cleanly.
You smell of the sea-green lace
of lichen that clothes your body -
solicitous, fragrant with seasons.

Old stone, you solid essence
of nothing at all but us -
our mass and substance
which slowly grinds down the bones
as we sit, sniffing,
and stare puzzled
at you who stand up.

SINGING BOWL

At the river edge is
the tree, over the water.
Mirrors of sunlight minnow its neck
in fast shoals that glow against wood.
It glugs as it swallows.

The light moves. I take this swim in willow infusion
under the water that's stoked by the earth –
my ears feel its talking: a full taut fuck:
a dark blind sound, a white noise, a
chop and drop, a chink and spool.

At the base of my throat is
the soft bowl which holds speaking.
Thumbs fit its hollow
I press: words rise to the surface
the small bowl empties and fills.

My life churns, channels
downs love
when it can, thirst-full.
Beads of light
fling, lodge and weather me

mother, trim, tether me,
and so I float without harm
around the willow's wet ankles.
Its corpse-pale leaves flit and patter
swallows dive the sky in handfuls like flung seeds.

Now I step down to the sea's falling scoop.
The island watches from its rims
I am alone
with its mass and spirit, the water clangs a depth charge,
climbs stickily and clings
to me: a needle suspended by solution.

The core tugs until I point sharp end down.
The soft bowl filters the breath of me
I push gasps from it
hums circle like bees –
human creature sounds, which drown quickly

in the green brine as
ah its lung inflates deflates with a sigh.
A sigh.

We fall and rise we fill and empty
rise and fall together.

The neat sieving sound as waves lick fine shingle and drain back.
The weightlessness. Being carried, then the heavy tread

into gravity, carrying my self
which carries the singing bowl

THE JOURNEY OF MILK

Reaches through dark lanes, fat rivers,
materialises fast.
Sucks and eddies at the tongue tip
draws you in to hold you close.

It flows in pale beside you now
with the ghost of your old age,
when you dial your mother's number
and she asks you how you've been.

CITY

In a cheap hotel in Portland
warped dank walls, blank jammed window,
scared to look inside the wardrobe,
I sleep in my clothes and ring you.

When I slip down the corridor
a slow creak groans the building
as if the weight could pull it down –
men unhappy, I suppose.

OILSKINS

Sudden
rain, in Basra,
which drenches yellow dust.
Newsmen run out to rescue their
cameras.

Colours
darken. A man
looks down at his curved palms –
they are painted with fresh blood, it's
sticky.

A plane
turns up now, points
straight down: a friendless bird,
a boy's finger shooting at dirt
for fun.

It sheds
Some little balls
of flash which float
and scatter, silently at first.
Someone

crouches
against a low
wall, on a roof, smoking.
The fire blinks and rubs him away,
takes him.

It's still
pouring. Some men
lower a friend, wrapped in
black plastic. He flops so flatly.
They're soaked.

Of all
the luck: a bomb
manages to hit some
graves. Bodies explode again from
steamed earth.

Three blocks
west, the newsmen
have found their yellow coats
and cluster under awnings, wait
and smoke.

Until
the rain stops, crowds
jostle and protect wet
heads with bags. Young ones peep through their
mum's legs.

THE POLYSTYRENE THEME PARK

They told us it had no meaning,
that there was no need for meaning
and meaning was meaningless.

Our teeth squeaked as we walked
through expanded oil product
moulded in the image of a good time:

a clumsy manifestation
of the fun that didn't occur.
Our feet silted and clogged,

the flakes filled our mouths, not sweet,
bland, a vengeance of ashtrays.
We knew no better, we meant no harm,

they told us no matter, you won't be alone
but our whispers hung in a cluttered dead desert
and knowing there's nothing, we remained alone.

TEA STRAINER

A silver strainer for filtering liquids was found buried with the body of the Queen/Priestess in the Royal tombs of Ur, from Mesopatamia in 2600 BC.

If you're falling
to be scooped by a net and held,
you think, for a second, and spun
suspended in a silver dip of cage
lights pricking through its grid
then to keep on falling –
to pour through
and leave your bones behind
and keep on falling –

is to be fathomless, to fall harder.

THE MIRROR IN THE PALACE IN BHUJ

is dim, air-blown
and cuts off our heads. Tired out from gazing back

it warps from the wall, pregnant with amber light.
                              Its full memory

absorbs no more now, has no opinion
of this century. It has retreated, passive as a lake.

We bend our knees to peer in, with the shiver
it gives me to look at a shipwreck through silt drift:

My clumsy salwar kamiz and baseball boots
swim through old fog to greet me.

The glass contains a record of the dead, it's
stained with staring and the unchanging backwards

walls; the floor cushions which line the room
and still sag from the Maharao's body.

The palace has a dancing room –a podium
rises out of empty water. The tiles

are eighteenth-century Dutch, in blue and white.
It is twelve months before the earthquake comes,

and you write to me, on butterfly-wing paper,
in your French-English: "Of the city, I am worried no more."

The mirror must have buckled and turned in
on itself, the reflections stacking up

under the cubed grey avalanche, like slides
of data, making strata.

It is six years before I can google it. My reflection looms over
the screen, which fills with an image of rubble.

The shapes pretend to slide back
where they came from when I leave, but etch the glass.

CLOUDS

Two drooping mountains
my eyelids. Below, my breath -
flame flickers and weaves.

Grey buzz and rattle -
Vodaphone, someone's son calls.
Corridors huddle.

Two sandcastles sink –
our particles float and stick,
dust waves choke the light.

Beyond my window
the handclap of two birds' flight
silent through this glass

Bald curve of platform -
a glimmer hangs above tracks,
next season twitching.

Leaves fling past the train,
golden stitches blowing by -
solemn air throws air.

They have sent more planes.
Razorcuts across washed sky
bleed white fluff for now

Long whistle tunnel:
pure darkness to stare into,
metal charge of earth.

Relief of finding
black velvet at the centre –
let me fall and fall.

DAYS IN

The trailings and curlings of your mind
skittered and clattered along the floor behind
your meandering hands, your webbed blue eyes
as you ambled through the dark house, crabwise.

Then jittered determined down the baking road
telling of how you saw what you heard
and thought what you saw
and heard what you thought. And thought about war.

Your hand repeats the journey to your mouth
with the cigarette which helps you breathe
as you pluck words from the Bible in bewilderment
and chew upon the matter of your mind. I send
off your prescription, and listen to your voices
as I clear dense papers from your room to make space.

CCTV

Wet headlights shine and stalk magnified figures
who crab to the screen, dripping black leather
down the street clammy-handed – this motion is constant
in the way they work, this Saturday night,
which,
dense with rain-bubbles that burst on the pavement,
shakes its unsteady, its rough strands open
like a curse: unfolding to all –
and within it they mooch, muck and buy the kit
to tilt their heads
very far black. One man, look,
with a coal beard and blanket hood, his framed face
like Jesus and Mary combined,
shadows away, shot-at, out of sight.

PAUL,

your veins –
you are heaving
silence into them
again,
which brings the white
worms of sweat
that shroud you, while you stagger and smooch

with the cocky lover
behind your eyelids:
the one who will make you
sleep in the rain,
the one who shoots a blurred alphabet through
your channels like a cold pistol.
The one you love.

BS 3

I come in to your city
and there you are, immediately
in a new car, passing me.
It isn't you, actually. It wouldn't be. It won't be.

Tonight the whole thing heaves around again.
From my small room I watch, and see
the suspension bridge, its lights a swinging
rope of pearls, the shadows
inching to bliss across the chasm
the suicides dropping from it like melting plastic.

At the foot of the garden, a square of window
cuts a yellow eye from the darkness. It holds a man,
its pupil, in a proper white shirt
at midnight. He washes up. Here in his old age
he begins to waltz, polishing a pan.
He covers the kitchen with his dance.

The shadows tick across the lights
from left to right:
in tower blocks. On the car bridge. A moth, a street lamp. A house –
the men in their boxes spanning the gulf,
sitting it out. Sirens gather pace
and scream incredible stories
across your city.

You live out there somewhere.
The gorge fills with souls slow and steadily
as drifts of leaves. They fall
through our linked, distracted hands.

KATHMANDU

The city's sky is stretched
and swollen, and the air
is thin. It nearly cracks the people.

Their houses lie in square mazes
with the fallen between, in dust.
Birds dance in time above.
Below them, warrens, lonely.

The sun peeps down, a lowered eyelid. Shuts.
I cannot see. I turn away, climb up.
I want to help you, weld us whole
with strength and warmth and amber glue.
But air is thin.

SAMHAIN

How the pumpkin changed
As soon as I completed
the circular sawing of its scalp
and lifted the lid away
by its tuft

with a suck

to peep in at orange membrane,
and smell fresh exposed flesh.
This was serious.
My hands had to burrow,
root up handfuls of hair
that slid with the flat seeds
living there,
and reach through the manhole
as it let the light inside
the dense mine of him.

I took a knife to the meat,
and carved blind. Little slices offered up,
I piled them
beside the soft matter of his core.
Skating, my blade stabbed rind -
it cleared with a pop into the empty head.

The handle slipped with its private slime.
My eyes scratched with fibres I hadn't guessed
could irritate:
new science.
I cut sharp features
into a side
creased with weathered patience -
the slow hardening it had managed,
and stretch marks it had to show,
and scuffings.

How easy it was to let the shapes out -
to punch deep chunks of skin
in, and hear them echo in there.

How you changed
when I dropped the flame
inside your hollowed self.
You laughed
with arched eyebrows,
pulsed with the flicker,
your ear-spirals pale
on the shadowed wall.
Exisiting, you forgave me
for primitive alchemy
and careless ripping

and thinking nothing of ceremony
which laces from darkness a pattern of light
and warms this room now that it is night.

NEW YEAR'S DAY BALLOONS

Eight of them. They gassed silently
over the yard this morning
drifting from the pub, beside the canal
where there was a corpse last year.

They muscled into the faded sepia branches
where a nest thickens the tree's centre,
and they'll stay there now, a clutch of dull eggs,
gun-metal grey, and brown-gold.
They bounce and squabble in the squally wind.
Three are limp. They clutch at the swollen heads of the others.

Last night the fireworks blew
the sky yellow.
You told me they spent a million pounds
on exploding the air with clouds of thunder.
Today the swollen things lodge in the ash tree,
and won't decay. They will sit there all day
every day, like a flock of murders.

IN THEIR GARDEN, AFTER THE OSTEOPATH

The ice has cracked and let the soft grass lift.
It's free to face the sun
and stretch, teased out like fleece,
tentative.
Its cells drift from roots as they warm.

Comes dusk. Dark garden
and sky light. As the stars swell
the thaw's new flow
happens upon the intense, digesting soil.
It moves in sudden space
at the foot of air.

This moment jostles in time
with all the others, scraping through the thought-pen.
The moon bowls into a mitt of ribbed cloud
and sinks us to a universe of total void.
Smitten by this dark,
eyes shut, I stand guard
while wind makes water roll like tears
released just now, today.

YOUR SCIENCE

This question of your faith – let me look:
your hat covers your head and lets in nothing.
So when the ice cracks like chip fat
and you fall through
inside the earth will glimmer nothing
and the sky will part with a stirring of nothing
damp dust will fray your throat
and you will lie in an empty hole forever.
Very bored. Fuck that. You move to feelings
wary and slow as an elephant's eye,
crusty with suicide residue –
I believe you've swallowed ivy which grunts and blinds you.
But cough it up, hold our hands,
make a truce with the lingering dark.

CIGARETTE, FARMYARD, 1 A.M.

And I am here.
So why do I blow smokescreens?
As if it's not enough
to stand on this ground
and tip my head to a map of lights
each one aligned
with different treasure marks.

My god, it's full of stars
and the air's a complicated musk
but I let my tongue fur with sand,
draw base fumes through the five points of me.
I am looking, and huge, and here.
The stars ring out like bells
I try to muffle them.

AT BLAKENEY POINT

By the flat edge of land
a ragged lattice of geese,
a family of some kind,
hauls over us.
It throws honks which clatter into the grey,
each bird a knot in a memory of lace.

As it passes, you and I discuss
netting a little one down:
guiding it to ground until
it walks between us.
Someone to take forward,
a node we could make,
a grid point.
It could go on, and overtake us.

Back in the car, we run through how we'd make it. Our breath
makes the cold air jostle and lean in, smudging the windows.

WHAT HAPPENED IN LITTLE TOR ORCHARD
"These apples will keep til apples come again."
Old Suffolk saying.

We lay down
in apple mash and nettles, pips shot from under us
my hands clasped the dock stalks, palms filling with their
juicy hollow snap, we ground against the template of the tree
and carefully changed our shape then a prick
to my wrist, a wasp – its little sting was hanging from my skin
and a blob of creamy goo at the top of it. We lanced the pain away
as the milk spread through my blood and turned it solid and hot, quickly,
you said,
before the poison spreads, as it will, and burns all night.
With the brown puckered skulls of the fruit
around us caved and exhaling, I wanted to say:

let grass mark your body

and earth inside me, this is solid and real –
when blossom comes, let's walk here, kicking at
the black husks which the frost bit. Let's keep seeding,
I didn't dare to say.

THE FISHERWOMAN IN THE PAINTING

I mined at the edges of grief
playing a dull and subtle hand:
blending fragments, taking cuttings,
cranking my gold from the water
like a smith, catching pale loot.

I used three ways to pray:
forecasting weather,
knitting,
inching forwards,
and thought I was ready

to be released in to blue sky,
but wasn't.
Light smattered across the years, identical
primroses curled in Easter sun,
my nets sucked and puddled –

the fish mouthing at me until
I would have been swallowed by
the void inside them. I decided
the truth was in the midden, the clay.
Next time round, I'd farm the earth.

Even if moss blew and cursed the wheat,
even if the cliffs ignited,
I would plant my feet on dry land –
away from these grey greedy lakes
who lift lips to a storm and drink it whole.

EDEN

See three full smacking spoonfuls of stout – drink it.
Lick smoke from the air as it idly ladles your way,
and use the tips of those cypresses to pick your teeth.

There is a space between the sun and the mountain –
Curl into it: don't be scared by impassivity or glare or age.
Teeter on your tiptoes like a fork spinning: angled and conducted.

Land on the city wall, sleep there a night – fit to it.
Now you are everything, so shrink or grow, take the form you like,
Pull the sky to you as a cloak. Shriek, swoop, and seize it.

HEADFIRST

The days when tears brew over all the time
– you are fine: just leaky and alive.
You watch snug rivers shine away along
the grass still minted with frost. The sunlit mast,
the poplars which stand together uncupping their hands,
the birds filling out the hollows as they peck together and
horses steady on heavy legs, breathing mist into substance
between themselves, their tender noses.

This started in the taxi to the station – the woman on the radio
reading from the papers: in Norfolk, a fake Iraqi village,
in which Prince Harry is being prepared
with the sounds of riots and calls to prayer.
The blackthorn is out already.
You are rushing through a plain suffused with light,
the animals mumble the surface, looking in
and you stare through scratched glass back at them.

THING

The coral is the song of the earth
that rises shaking in notes
and settles to a threaded pattern
of waving holes in water

or, older, lies under land
holding love in laced plates
a long time here.

FOR MY SISTER'S EIGHTEENTH

In my dream I wrote a sonnet
for your birthday, looking down at you asleep –
you were fourteen or four, deeply tucked up,
keeping warm.   My rose-like.

I wrote of your eyebrows, how their delicate
chocolate line has not changed since I first
encountered you, at twenty minutes old.
And of the fine green that flickers your eyelid –

how that vein tells the tale of you.

How I tried to teach you to waltz, though I did not know how.
And guaranteed you my protection although I could not.

I wanted to describe
your grace, your wide shoulders, the joy of your breath
the happiness it has given me that you are here.

BILLACK'S BONES

As you see, I am burning.
Here, my heart is cracked all apart: snap
off the pieces and
dip them into the honey
which brims over and runs
through me, I promise you.
Sit and listen if you like:

this is a story. I was born.

The electricity spun me out. I wound
through sky, I sparked
as I bounced off rocks.
I went head over heels, a human reel
down a seedy gully. Gold net blew behind me.
I tumbled in grace, in the rays of the sun
but spasmodic and flung.
I was not natural.
My life had begun.

They tell me

the bones formed a clump of matter moving through space:
spun like a bow tie
motioned through clear air, became immersed.
It drifted down river, clunked against banks,
watched by daisy-grazing goats with yellow mirror eyes.
Suspended not held, it was pushed
and turned. Bubbles nibbled and cast it
way down the stream. Bumping,
tied to the bends.

I met the bones at the bottom,
a jacket to a hanger.
We settled in to walk together pretty well.

But just now, I am burning.
I try my hand with a stick, help the fragments shoot about.
Black atoms sail out spark-sheathed and disguised
over the village.
My days fly round the houses in new dust;
they lie in wait in puddles as the school bus splashes past.
Feel free to grind my bones to make your bread –
I fold in on myself, of carbon,
let the flames lick me as clean as knives,
as I watch the page be taken, the words become un-spoken.

CODA

Listen to the deep

                    heartbeat

inside your ribs

           and let yourself lift to the high

    lake of the sky, to control this thud,

        this thud thud thud

        of foot and chest

which lures you awake

although you are   still sleeping.

There is no language to explain -

      destroy this paper: chew it up,

           spit out the lump

               and swallow.

             Breathe.

Joanna Guthrie was born in London in 1970, and grew up near Diss, on the Norfolk-Suffolk border.

She has written since childhood, and has been published as a poet for the last 10 years.

In between travelling and idling, she has done various jobs, most notably in homelessness and mental health. She completed an MA in Creative Writing in 2006, from the University of Exeter.

Last year she was one of three people shortlisted in the Creative Non-Fiction category of New Writing Partnership's New Writing Ventures 2006; she is currently working on a political travelogue/memoir as a result of this, with the support of a Grant from the Arts Council. After a decade living in the West Country, she's currently living in Norwich.